D'EUX & OTHER SORROWS

ALSO BY LAURIE BYRO

La Dogaressa & Other Poems
Bloomsberries and Other Curiosities
Wonder
Gertrude Stein's Salon and Other Legends
Luna

D'eux & Other Sorrows

Laurie Byro

Cowboy Buddha Publishing, LLC
Benton, Arkansas

D'eux & Other Sorrows

Copyright © 2019 by Laurie Byro

No part of this book may be reproduced or transmitted in any form or by any means, electronic or mechanical, including photocopy, recording, or any information storage or retrieval system, without permission in writing from the author or their agents, except by a reviewer to be printed in a magazine or newspaper, or electronically transmitted on radio or television.

Cowboy Buddha Publishing, LLC
Benton, Arkansas
www.cowbubpub.com

Book design & layout by Jessica Dyer
Cover and interior art by Michael Byro: Byroart
COVER: *"Starry Night on the Rhone"* in Pointillism
PG 4: *"Dr. Gachet"* in Pointillism
PG 22: *"Café Terrace at Night"* in Pointillism
PG 32: *"Isadora in Corfu"* in Pointillism
PG 38: *"Old Man Grieving"* in Pointillism
PG 81: *"Night Crows"* in Pointillism

Publishing logo by Ted Nichols
First Edition: May 2019

Cowboy Buddha Publishing is a boutique publishing company which seeks to foster adventurous spirits and the sharing of wisdom. To find out more, visit our website at www.cowbudpub.com or email cowbudpub@gmail.com.

ISBN 978-0-9994795-1-3

For Helen Anna
Who, like the stars, is always there...

In high summer, dragonflies teach us about safety and risk,
but scare us with their shifty garnet or tourmaline eyes. Each month,
according to our custom, we women form a circle and tell each

other stories. Wise old Mother, she sweeps the kitchen floor,
braids the hair of one of us, tucks a handkerchief into
the pocket of another. The hearth is ablaze tonight,

it makes the stars all but disappear, it has made us all
go silent. Still we form a circle with her always at the center.
Still we manage to continue even when she is safe at home.

Contents

Introduction 1

The Other Vincent 7

Raven 8

Model 9

Paradise 10

Blue Requires Yellow 11

Poison Wood (Sien Nursing Baby 1883) 13

Gauguin Sends Vincent a Warning 14

Letter From Marie Ginoux 15

Blue Heron 16

Talk Before Sleep 17

Crows 18

Villanelle With Vincent 19

The Ghost of Vincent Van Gogh Speaks to Chin-yeh Chi 20

The Ghost Visits Gertrude Stein 21

The Familiar 25

Isadora at 27 Dances To Tchaikovsky 26

Water Study: Iris and Lily's Gift of Prophecy *28*

Isadora *29*

Singer Sewing Machine *30*

The Seine *31*

Deirdre Beatrice Craig *32*

Samhain Taroc *34*

Corfu Ash *36*

A Red Scarf *37*

OTHER SORROWS:

A Song of Heart Break *41*

Lies For Icarus's Mother *42*

The Birds That Lay Down For Icarus *43*

Icarus's Sister *44*

Cleopatra's Song *45*

Katharine Hamlet Of Avon Sings Herself to Sleep *46*

Dreams of the Evil Step-Mother *47*

The Best Sister of Wyrd *49*

Soldiers *50*

Shape-shifting For Frida Kahlo *51*

Christmas Tree *54*

Mask	*57*
LoveSong	*58*
The Ghost of Shura Speaks	*60*
Eating Crow	*61*
Devon Song	*62*
Full Fathom Five	*63*
The Ghost of Branwell Drinks Bitter	*64*
Shadows	*66*
Rose La Touche	*67*
The Year Without a Summer, Poems for Fanny Godwin	*68*
Sarah Bernhardt's Missing Leg	*71*
For Angel Claire	*73*
An Ocean As a Deity	*75*
Day of the Dead	*76*
Horse Thunder	*78*
The Girl From The North Country Speaks	*79*
George in Grackles	*80*
ABOUT THE AUTHOR	*83*
ACKNOWLEDGMENTS	*85*

INTRODUCTION:

From Their Sorrow, Our Joy

Laurie Byro must have a room of her own, maybe several—how else could she dream her way into the 1800s and bring it so vividly to life. These poems equal the best lyricism of that time and any other. I love a poet who seems to say, *historians tell us what these great figures did, but I think I know what they felt.* And so, this book becomes a prolonged dream made from the basic concrete facts of former times.

In the first section, several portraits are painted: Vincent and Theo Van Gogh, Paul Gauguin, Gertrude Stein, Isadora Duncan, and more—lives active during the same approximate time period. Each heart finds a home in these poems, showing how pain is endowed with a beauty that only poetry can understand.

In poems from "A Grief Tableau," Theo Van Gogh despairs of the blood on Vincent's pillow— Model Marie Ginoux begs Theo to tell Vincent to reject Gauguin: "I didn't like him. He looks at me and all women in a boorish disgusting way…"— Vincent implores Dr. Gachet to let him keep his madness—Can we agree that the best poetry is high literary gossip? And how many of us can turn away from poems, juicy, tantalizing and imagistic.

Byro enters her artists' extreme visions, reinforcing the best and worst in their lives. Her elegant lines, and the mysterious way she creates tranquility and intensity are called "craft." I don't like that word either, but it's the only way we can describe the writing. This poet doesn't race with the clock; she carefully unravels her thoughts to design, in phrase and clause, color, sight and sound, exact situations and scenes. These poems are written in real time; here and now; and with her innovations, we feel we're meeting these subjects for the first time.

This scholar has a solid grip on the 19th and 20th century art worlds. In Section 2, "Other Sorrows," poems are inspired by Sarah Bernhardt, Bob Dylan, Ted Hughes, Sylvia Plath, Frida Kahlo, and Percy Bysshe Shelley, among others. In the Shelley poem, "The Year Without a Summer: For Fanny Godwin" Byro creates the story of Mary Shelley's half-sister in a few sweet stanzas. It is the only poem in existence, I believe, about tragic Fanny. Also, illuminating the least celebrated, Byro writes about Luz Corral de Villa, wife of the Mexican revolutionist, Pancho Villa.

This entire collection is a journey of change; telling us the poet is always watching history, engaging, looking for creative satisfaction. These inventions about literary icons bang headfirst against an engine already in motion. Yet Byro's not afraid; she describes human endeavors in a new light, saying, *what is the central issue here, what is the meaning, where is the spirit,* then she brings her own beautiful language and experience, created by nature, to document the imagined. As a patron of language, Laurie Byro's odyssey with art and history is the real story here. This book of poems wins a beauty contest.

– Grace Cavalieri, *Maryland Poet Laureate*

A Grief Tableau The First:

"The sadness will last forever." – Vincent Van Gogh

THE OTHER VINCENT

Theo, I never told you or our parents that the other Vincent, the one
who was born dead whispers to me from the dark cloak he wears as he

grows tall like a shadow on the days I am alone. When I look out
at the Rhone, he walks toward me carrying his armful of stars.

They are really chrysanthemums, don't tell him I know, but in his hands
they glow off the water like sticks of fire. Is he preparing a pyre

for the second Vincent? Do you miss him like I do? Little stranger, he died
without sin. He was good at mathematics, he was smart at school. He may

have been a priest so often he hears my confession. I worry for his ears
in frost. He glows as if he is covered in snowy moths. I was his best brother.

He never complains like you about my voices. You take after Mother
in worry. Theo, sadly, I am again in need of certain colors. Please send

as you can, bolts of canvas and tubes. You can help me match my moods:
azure and grey for dreary Wednesday, cornflower, cobalt, aquamarine. Oh

that glorious gold of angels. Oh the sooty overcoats of crows, of brothers.
There are brothers to spare, angels everywhere. You are my favorite, really.

Raven

*"I always think that the best way to know God
is to love many things."* – Vincent Van Gogh

When the first midnight-blue raven took off,
a wild parasol, shielding the others from too bright sun,
I was drawn across the river into my new life.
I knew nothing could console me, not their angelic

wings anointing the other side, as they embrace
the future, leaving me behind watching them
in wonder. I'll not ask for the impossible, I was
raised on them as charity and they could be like that:

chariots, drawing me out of my breath, all mistakes
left behind. But who would imagine this effortless escape?
What God draws them into this sky, abandoning

the world this way, a tiny clump of madness
turning and resting with little consequence. And me,
with whatever passed between us; no hint of reproach.

MODEL

"Painting demands an intelligent model." – Vincent Van Gogh

You think it will last, the painter
his light suffusing you with tired legends—
pale pinks and lilac-tinged sunsets
night-blooming Cereus women
that smell of turpentine.

He tells you that pears and oranges
taste sweetest when sucked off the tendrils
of a lover's hair.

You narrow your eyes, he dabs
and smears a teal sky.
He grows impatient as you sit, tweaks
a nipple, tells you to concentrate
on a point beyond, on a sunset.

Tonight I can't sleep for
watching your arms as you paint me—
the whorls of hair on your wrist, electric.

I roll out our old blankets
November chill
under a lady-slipper moon.

I take off all but your silver
as I dismantle the old easel.

Cross legged on cotton batting
I peel the moon out of yesterday.
A lovely full breasted orange—
I remember sweetness,
slice by slice.

Paradise

"Life being what it is, one dreams of revenge." – Paul Gauguin

Paul Gauguin tells me to begin by counting sheep, and so
one Cotswold, one Coopworth but after a short time I am distracted.

I start over with a ram, a mongoose, a chicken then a conch
that spills secrets and awakens me with its chatter.

A worm bounces off each spiral, each swirl of pink. Paul
Gauguin isn't pleased with our progress. I start over by counting

orchids, one Moth, one Dancing-lady, yet somehow instead I land
inside a frame of the Dutchman. As the stars descend like madness,

Vincent tells me not to share this with anyone. A blue spotted dog
barks at a Chagall-goat, its horns stirring ivy-green moons. His ear

listens closely to each confession, separated as it is by a thief
who carries a knife. It tucks-in under blood red petals

in a Tahitian bowl, its bed, sea glass. All night and then the next,
angry Birds of Paradise stand guard summoning poetry, echoing stars.

BLUE REQUIRES YELLOW

*"Art is either plagiarism or revolution;
but I owe something to Vincent Van Gogh."* – Paul Gauguin

The painter returns as promised,
his canvasses wet with humidity;
island women drip off his brush.

He lines them up around the room.
It is January, a monochromatic season.
No snow adorns the trees, a cloudy
night with no star to follow and you pretend

to be delighted. Each banana laden tree,
parrots the color of apricots, of coral,
and those women each radiant garden—
the plum cheeked Martiniquais, hair adorned
like a queen, pink fuchsia woven into rags,
her breasts, two tropical birds.
In other paintings, you see her succulent belly,
mysterious with pregnancy, and imagine
holding a knife like his brush
to slice her open, to see the newborn's eyes.

As he expects a response, you
concentrate on her nipples, how they
have darkened—the fuchsia that once
matched her flower adorned hair, now
large brown coffee beans.

Later when he swirls his tongue in patterns
of orchids like he once painted on your
boyish flatness, he uses it to probe your navel.
Far off, you hear rainfall, a baby cry,
the sigh of palm trees, the click of bamboo lulling
fluttering eyelashes to sleep.

His penis wags at you like something you hardly
remember, a greedy snake, cruelly poisonous.

Your animal teeth are dangerously sharp.
Posing for him in moonlight, you wonder
if by morning he will get the colors
exactly right—your sleek mongoose body,
your bloodstained teeth.

Poison Wood (Sien Nursing Baby 1883)

"Last winter I met a pregnant woman (Sien), deserted by the man whose child she carried. The woman is now attached to me like a tame dove."
– Vincent Van Gogh

For nine months, almost ten, I sip
your poison. It grows in my belly, pushing

my buttons out. My ears are two perfect
fetuses that curl around my head. Your bed

fills with stories, some call them lies. I leave
them in the forest, they root as orchids.

They are the kind that thrive on blood and smell
like musk. The forest floor is littered

with sooty fireflies so I sweep them into a pile
to feed to your exotics. My hair coils into

striped snakes that hiss at these lovely carnivores.
These beautiful creatures miss our messy

bed. Under a lady-slipper moon, I shake off
all of your trances. The Gods are gone tonight.

Your daughters and I are sober and real.
We rid ourselves of you; we dance with ghosts.

They bow and we curtsy. The moon, a thin
and shallow spoon, ladles broth to our lips.

Gauguin Sends Vincent a Warning

When Paul Gauguin wrote, I tried to be indifferent to the lure
of orchids, the scent of yellow butterflies, pollen still dusting their wings.

Then he described the taste of cinnamon skin and it enchanted me.
Afterwards I noticed their black ember eyes following me around

the room, outside through the barren stalks of corn. I asked each firefly
should I encroach upon his Eden? I wrote him back describing the ashes

that would one day replace my own body. I held a jar that would soon
trap me dull and sooty. I was certain I would no longer be a jar of lava

jewels, these fireflies I released to the crows to feast on would betray
me. Some nights, when there is a salty sky, I cross the sea and enter

his dark jungle. I slide down the cinnamon skin bark of a tree. No woman
ever really wanted me. My ribs and lightning whip body is a green brush

darting among wild nights. He had known all this and warned me not to
waste my precious days. I could shrug off this tired life as he had done,

leave it behind like a tattered robe, no longer wanting to be claimed,
not important enough for the lonely crows to fight over.

Letter From Marie Ginoux

Theo, not to frighten you for I admire your brother. It is a friendship
close to love. That rascal Paul Gauguin has arrived. Your brother

summoned him and it is a complete disaster. Please convince him
to leave; beg Vincent to give up his obsession of a colony of artists.

Gauguin is not a companion of the bosom, it is an attraction of opposites.
I repeat it is a failure. I have been posing for Vincent as an excuse to give

him food, he will pay by painting me. It is no sacrifice, your brother
has the gift of a compassionate heart as well as art yet he insists that this

ruffian paints me, too. I don't like him. He looks at me and all women
in a boorish disgusting way. I take his money for the cafe. But I want

him to move on. Your brother is agitated, it is all I can do to make him eat.
When he paints the stars falling, I believe I could catch one in my hands.

Can't you see the stars illuminating his frenetic bird like frame? I pray
for God to save him. Like all holy men he works all night. When I rise

early to make that day's bread for my cafe, I sing his name and all
their names, those of the sick and suffering into the fragrant morning.

Blue Heron

"Grant that we may meet her on our path, grant that one day Mrs. Van Gogh may sit before us in the carriage." – Theo Van Gogh

The story goes that the painter from Holland hired her
as his model. She was as untouched by him as the blue
heron they'd seen asleep with its head under its wing.
The couple slept side by side for many months

and then the painter died. The heron, or probably one
of its descendants, rose like a parasol and glided
over the banks of the Rhone where it stood
like a sentinel beside the iris blanketed pond.

His dreamscapes peeled off the water in all shades
of blue for each night she slept next to him but would
not agree to marry. Fog, thick as tempura, settled around

the old house where inside the woman dreams of Delft
blue eyes. Pipes creak. An early painting of her seems
to sigh and moan, startling spiders, displacing dust.

TALK BEFORE SLEEP

Vincent, last night sharing your pillow, I tried to disappear into your sleep.
I am shaken by the blood dripping into the holster that once held your ear.
Does it excite you to damage yourself, make yourself unfit for your assured

success? Dear Brother, your work is sublime, but you are becoming
the madman of Arles, and not the genius of the palette. Genius

is the word most often on the lips of our friends, Georges and Henri.
Gauguin is an ass, paint from memory, paint from present, just paint
and ignore his bohemian whore-life. I do believe he struck you

with his knife. But your ear? After you bizarrely circumcised yourself,
I asked the doctors what does this mean? You adore women, your flowers

are your woman but you destroyed your appeal. Why? Not to hear
those evil voices? To savage a woman's secret place? Was it to bring
petals to a whore? Were you trying to restore their virtue? You must stop.

Vincent, you must stop destroying parts of yourself. This will not cure you
of your madness, you are not removing your madness. As you recalled

as we drifted off to sleep in hospital, we were again skating beneath
the windmills in Laakmolen. Your blank canvas is a memory plate
of our childhood. You must fill this plate and leech yourself of the poison

in your soul. Father forgives you, become the son he wanted.
Be the perfect one, he will soon have another Vincent to love. Vincent,

you clamor on about my unborn son with his tiny ears. He hears
his Uncle. He loves his Uncle. All the paint you want, Brother,
all the paint you need and forever. I promise, just please stop hurting us.

Crows

Dr. Gachet, you tell me my crows are thieves and dirty scavengers,
that you will rid me of my obsession with them. If you are to cure me
of my madness, kindly leave the birds out. They are my truest friends.

They want nothing of me but to share my bread and my company.
The leader, I call him Paul Gauguin, struts in his black mourning coat,
issuing orders. He is sly and tricks us into obedience. The others

are angels you see, drawn to the beauty of soot. They don't understand
their value in the world. I have invented my own world as God invented his.
There is Sien who never tempts me with her body, her boa of darkness.

There is Claude Monet, the fat one, who only wishes to make water ripple
off his sword. He makes lilies speak to each other and that is not delusion.
Can't you hear them? They love me. Can't you see the mistake of curing me,

of killing them off in my memory? My women are sunflowers, their heavy
hated grace, their sleepy eyes. It is my will to make them beautiful. Neither
a blossom nor a bee will shun me. They don't turn away from my perfume.

This is not madness, doctor, only acceptance. My angels are freaks, unaware
of their perfect bodies and lovely souls. What if they come to me as a murder
of crows? If my lovers are chaste and still as petals, who are you to turn me

into a sane man? I shall cut off my other ear so as not to hear you scold me
into mediocrity. You and Theo will nag me to death. You are wrong to think
I am invisible to the universe. I am Vincent. I need no other name.

Villanelle with Vincent

And then Van Gogh learned that matadors will cut off the ear of a bull to show courage and present it to their lady...

A matador can never be afraid
unless his pride is given to the light.
And thus dear Vincent knew the price he'd paid.

For company and love, he always prayed.
He prayed soft fields would dazzle him with light.
A matador can never be afraid.

And with a final thrust his future made.
A swagger as he dances near the light.
And then poor Vincent knew the price he'd paid.

He gave his lady-love the gift he'd made.
It glistened like a star in morning light.
A matador can never be afraid.

In France, he learned of matadors who made
a show of taming passion with a fight.
Was then our Vincent knew the price he paid.

Crow-sunflower, he watched the colors fade.
A swirling cape, a star, both made of light.
And then dear Vincent knew the price he paid.
A matador must never be afraid.

The Ghost of Vincent Van Gogh Speaks to Chin-yeh Chi

You have failed me with your empty easel,
your brushes sitting motionless,
like the bird who watched stars
from the asylum window.

Dr. Gachet said pay him no mind,
but he told me many odd things
about the universe, about stars colliding
with the earth. I tried to paint them,
I tried to capture that harbinger of death.
Instead I became giddy with the idea
of making black strokes with his feet,
like an Oriental master.

Chin-yeh Chi, you are a failed painter,
with your strange, unborn dreams.
I am writing to Theo with an idea
of an artist without paint,
who will record these dreams
into beautiful blank pages.

> The bird flew off
> colliding with a star
> and the dry dust of the winter garden
> receives each fallen feather
> like black rain-drops.

Upon awaking, Chin-yeh Chi
writes down this entire painting
with his finest camel hair brush.

The Ghost Visits Gertrude Stein

I have watched you
and the one you call Alice
during the black petals of sleep,
when all hardness leaves your faces.

There is a field of tulips not far
from the town I lived in as a boy,
with ragged dark flowers.
The spongy earth
still makes these strong and odd,
almost devoid of beauty,
similarly different
from their pastel companions.

Most of my companions are whores.
If I want a woman, I give up
the few guilders set aside for bread
or paint—I've taken the one with lice,
with that violet birthmark staining her cheek.

You are husband to her with your lips.
Your woman's body under those suits
you wear, the edges of your petals
give off luminous sparks,
so strangely you make fire.

If you look closely at my paintings,
you will know my women.
Their proud erect beauty,
their heavy-headed grace.

Each Iris, each Sunflower
who has turned from us.

The Second:

"For the first time since their death, I felt I was not alone."
— Isadora Duncan

The Familiar

You weren't certain of the hour she screamed mercy
under a gibbous moon. A homely wrinkled piece

of sin—the hobo-light winked as you straightened a fist,
saying, *it's a boy*. Now you are gone to another
loitering angel. She is a sylph like the mist that rises

off a lake. I am lost in a field that crackles with frost.
Flickering flames of creatures join me while I search

constellations for a map of our old life. I give myself up
to their magic to make us disappear. I barter
with a white rabbit in a bucket of midnight,

a hunched 'possum as he sifts through the neighborhood
trash. I enter their fiery eyes while you shudder.

Your pupils widen, you ogle the moon as it rises
over her head. When you come back and find me gone,
you will unclench your fist. You will slice windfall apples

and greet a new generation of thieves. Meanwhile, you dance
your tired dance, help her unbutton a buttermilk

tinted blouse. Tonight, it lays over the back of a chair
like a sleek rabbit while a thousand miles away
I hang my pointed hat on the moon.

Isadora at 27 Dances To Tchaikovsky

Because she was not awkward,
because she becomes a spun-sugar baby, a black
widow in a glittering
web, because
she transports them, because
she stands out like the purple eye
in the delicacy of a Queen Anne's Lace
flower, them the pearl shell, the mother
of the luminous lake pearl
and because she thought the dance was Tarantella,
never ever understood—

pushed up against it like a train heading
into snowy Moscow with those Russian wolves
howling outside her window
and she breathing the blast
of coal smoke and exhaling strings
of sweet gas, the floss of cotton candy,
she rubs against his arm like a spotting
cat, noticing the dark whorls of hair, the eight-legged
slip into tyranny.

Her taut, tight controlled body
just the way he likes it, zippered inside
itself, a secret under togas, a dance towards
his white light, a six pointed
star, not cocaine white or holy but because
he was the teacher and she the pupil
and because she slips inside
his skin, minds the illumination
of his ghost preacher

in and out and in
and out and through his incarnations
and because
her skin has begun to peel, to shed off
into a pile of sawdust
he blows her onto the floor where she becomes
the grit under all the fancy soles,
the stilettos and the boot heels,
the brave and naked toes.

Water Study: Iris and Lily's Gift of Prophecy

You, who I may have invented, summoned
from the night, dazzled by the light from the stars,
mirrored into the bowl I leave beside my bed, return

to the lake. Something about the water, the smell
of turtles, or was it the lake itself that called you back?
Irises chatter among themselves, captured by words

you've rehearsed, by the flutter of dragonflies' wings.
The Lady of Shalott, or so the story goes, weaves eternally
a reflection trapped inside her mirror and as spells break,

I tear the cord from the soil. I have smuggled you
to the glass where you coil the bowl like a wild braid,
to wait with me for someone who never appears. Lily,

in the glass bowl murmurs all night, recalling dragons,
a memory of webbed-wings over her head, flashing eyes,
blood-red flight and only the tiniest glimpse of a hand

with silver rings. She counts torn clouds, surrounded by glass,
a cord slinking over the rim and back to the river. I wonder
if you are gone for good this time, banished or forsaken,

in between bright sun and sooty wings. I wonder if they've shattered
you out of glass, stars burning on my cheeks, water rushing
back to water, all women weep: all women carry the sea inside them.

Isadora

"Affectations can be dangerous." – Gertrude Stein

The rain came down like a dance. Trees toss off their
silver needles like a dervish; a woman gets caught
up in the tarantella of her candles. She peers into the Book

of Thoth. She shuffles her men in the same way the cards
appear: knight, serf, jester and hermit. The rain
has lived through its troubles. The rain has gathered its

coupling creatures and ridden them through the storm.
The cards talk among themselves when no one is looking.
She is falling in love with another man. Still he covers

her body with the sweetness of warm rain. The downpour
is a grand *fouetté*. The Seine and the Thames are swelling
to their ninth month. She faces the card that is placed upside

down on the table, the Nine of Pentacles. The falcon
on the woman's hand indicates the taming of her animal nature.
She is more than a clever bitch, a braying donkey, the cock

will crow at dawn when she is just trembling off to sleep.
The rain is relentless, it floats swirling scarves set loose through
the streets where she has danced barefoot, blood dripping

off her toes. Rain wraps its tendrils of lacy shawls
around her shoulders. She will shrug it off along
with the tinkling of the drowned children's voices in the river.

She will say goodbye to the messy nests of magpies,
the sheen and buzz of bottle necks; gauzy blue-silk
rain that wraps her body fit to bursting through its skin.

Singer Sewing Machine

"I have come to help you. What can I do?" – Paris Singer to Isadora Duncan

I am forever hers.

I clasp her bodice with a vibrating gasp, my arm entraps her
by my spidery fortune, my arduous threads. Imagine nine hundred
soldiers, each stitching her a dowry, the time this has afforded her to love

me. All things are possible. The money I have earned for her, the hope
chest I have filled, can I help it that I inherited much, given my fearless

disposition? This is more than mechanical. We have wedded our fortunes.
She can ride me like a Greek bull onto stage. She doesn't need much.

I am her string of pearls, I am the diaphanous ardor she wears
so immodestly. She shrugs me off like a costume. I support her in all things,
freedom is a curse she shares with Lady Liberty. The expense of busks,

the blood shed for beauty. The waste of stays and pins, the vanity
of buttons. Long ago, I made a promise to her. I released her, nobody
not even raindrops have such perfect toes. She becomes a waterfall;

she becomes an ocean. Tunics and batting, we are forever embroiled.
She is a scarlet bird driven from my nest to the wooden floor.

The Seine

"You were once wild here. Don't let them tame you." – Isadora Duncan

My kingdom is speed and light; my mansion, rocks tumbling, glass settling in. Romantically, I love each bride: weeds for hair, moss for eyes, shells for spine. I am Ophelia rising. April is the suicide month, nine months after summer.

You must know I delight in the play of children. I am eternally their mother, I am grateful and restless. The future is here now, the frothy minutes, a graveyard to the past. The thought of pockets filled with stones,

and I, a bride groom to them, makes me gasp. I can't be sentimental. They become part of me, they spare fish and turtles being hungry. Would you expect me to give up my future for them? Imagine

the sounds of them keening to me at night, it is a miracle I don't take them all to heart. Even when languid I like to cause mischief. I've never met a dragonfly I didn't like. Don't list their names like some

wet poet, the more I gather to me, the more important I become. I speak all languages: *Aidez-moi, hilfe, Aiuto*. When the mist rises off me I could be every single one of them. Watch them float over me

and try to return to their past. When I am not weary of being held accountable, I taunt their mother: *Patrick, Deirdre, L'Inconnue de la Seine*.

DEIRDRE BEATRICE CRAIG

"I am here in a villa by the sea dying of despair." – Isadora Duncan

Mama, I held Patrick's hand tight just as you taught me when crossing the street because the water was cold and I was scared. The river

rushed over us like a blurry dream. The fish swimming past were angels. Though I could not speak, I mouthed to Patrick:

Don't be afraid. I thought, "We are going to a beautiful place where mermaids will comb and braid my hair. We will never worry

and always play." When I looked up through the tangled water, at the sky, I could see lilies and frogs. Damselflies and dragons became

bright cobwebbed light, just like their wings. Oh, that light. It lit up the turquoise blue sky and I mouthed to Patrick: *Don't be afraid.*

Heaven was pulling us into its arms just like you did, Mama. Mama, this place is so pretty, a world without end. Why do

the cobwebs in the angel's wings seem to disturb the light?

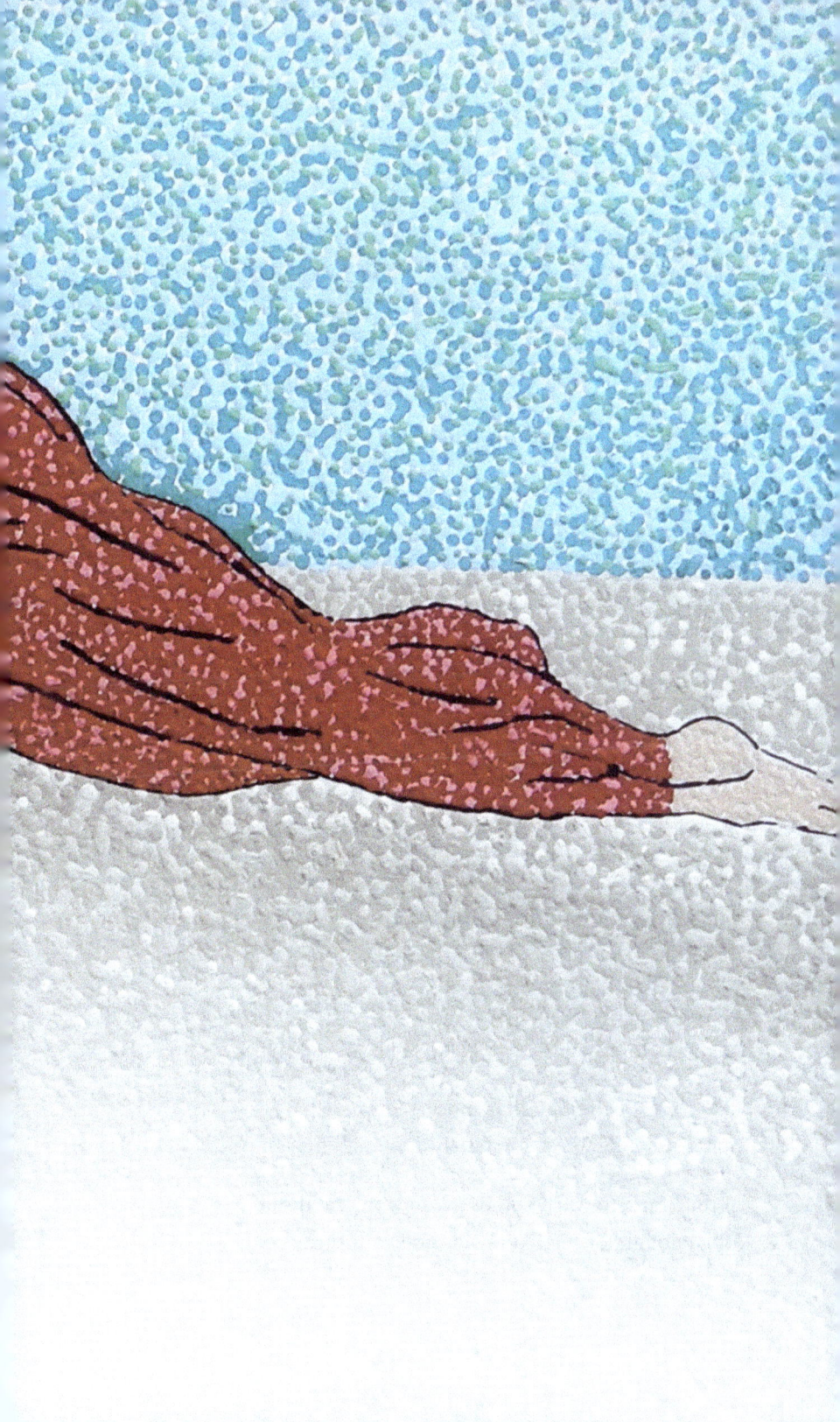

Samhain Taroc

"Perhaps he was a bit different from other people, but what really sympathetic person is not a little mad?" – Isadora Duncan

Inside the cabinet that still sticks when it's humid,
you wait inside a deck of cards just as I thought

we were through playing games. A monk shuffles
through his meditations in silence. I cut the deck

as fall turns into itself in its own way, unable
to change its vision to satisfy me. I spread our lives

all over the floor. Cross-legged, Corfu-sun mad,
I am a grubby queen, loyal but not faithful, my braid

something you would tear to keep as a tributary
to you. A hermit queues up to lead the procession

of dead. His heart is a winter hive that I have
scraped free of sticky honey. It's the time of year,

when clothes are rummaged through and bagged
for the poor. I can't bear to lose the last scraps

of your smell. I watch your breath rise in the morning.
Nights before I fall asleep, I lose sight of your masked

face. The dead hold their shoes and tiptoe past
our beds while we sleep. Lately, I light all the lamps

in the house to warn you off. You won't hold still
long enough for me to crawl inside your dusty coat

and release your demons into the wild air. As I finish
my supper, you place a piece of bread onto my tongue.

I spread the cards to reveal a better future. Tonight,
I will stuff your patched flannel shirt with leaves

in their patterns of splattered blood. I'll surround you
with every hanged man in the deck and force

our hand. Tomorrow, I will sit with you
as we doze on the porch. The buttons I've sewn on

for your eyes will glitter madly as if you know
for certain what will become of us.

Corfu Ash

"The Dance is love, it is only love, it alone, and that is enough..."
— Isadora Duncan

Maybe it was the full moon, a Corfu-blue eye, reminding me
that the river floods, roofs lose their tile and leak, children drown, children
go into a river to play. A full moon, any moon at all reminds me,

and rain, blue pelting tears: a lamp, a child crying. She is obsessed
with the taroc, they whisper, she is drunk with mother's love.

But what they didn't know is that instead of bringing their ashes
to the beach of Corfu like I said, I hoarded them and pretended
the leavings from an English grate was them. While on this island, waiting

for peace and their father, the moon swelled like my belly did once.
I ate them and drank them down.

It was easy as sticking your tongue out for snow. The marmalade,
the chicken and potatoes with garlic, I seasoned my days with them.

I sucked them through a straw. In my tea, in my wine, in my toast with jam,
in my throat.

I loved them.

Then I knew, looking up, that the moon: she was leaving me, too, in slivers,
night after restless night, drop by bleeding drop. Until there would be

nothing left when I drink my last bottle of Ahiri,
when I finish them.

A RED SCARF

"Je vais à l'amour. (I go to love)." – Isadora Duncan

I only wanted to be a cardinal, landing
on the white shoulders of a lady.
I was never a slash of blood, never a ghost

gathering pieces of a heart. But when
she brought me on stage, I got the taste
of a thunderous moment. It seemed

like a kind of destiny. It seemed like
I made a pact with a silent assassin. And I was
summoned somehow to always be with her.

OTHER SORROWS:

*"Someone I loved once gave me a box full of darkness.
It took me years to understand that this, too, was a gift."*
— Mary Oliver, Thirst

Song of Heartbreak
(for Icarus)

I. The Wanting (A Chorus)

Why then did you hunger?
   I wasn't sure of sorrow.

Tell us how his flesh felt?
   It felt like angels singing.

How then did you love him?
   With every beat and measure.

How then can you leave him?
   He wasn't mine for staying.

II. The Release (A Chorus)

How was it that you found him?
   I found his broken body.

What was sunshine to you?
   It was my only rival.

How then did you know him?
   I knew him by my heartbeat.

What now of his ashes?
   I bathe my body in them.

Lies for Icarus's Mother

We all have one spare boy to lose. I collect feathers
along a wooded lane: yellow finch, gold peso coins

on white, blue as midnight on a meerschaum pipe.
If I can trick the clouds into holding on to us,

if I can choke the piebald mouse gnawing roots
that snake under the old lightning split tree,

I will bring him my best porcelain flowered cup,
filled to the top with lapsang souchong tea.

He will land at our feet so gracefully that he will not
spill a drop. I note the spray of blood and the broken

shell of another creature's child. I gather silver plumes
to slip into your purse so you can spend them wisely

in your old age. Some days you have to make
your own luck. We sip sweet pomegranate wine

in the Mermaid Café. We take turns dancing
when the most seductive siren fails to lure him to her bed

of ravenous waves. Sap runs down the limbs
of pine trees and one last abandoned feather completes

my cache. Somewhere his father urges and repeats.
Tomorrow he will leave us for one quick hour.

Tufts of snowy owls fall from my pockets, birds peck
my liar's mouth like it's a blood thirsty worm.

THE BIRDS THAT LAY DOWN FOR ICARUS

Cormorants conspire to peck each other
to death to furnish him with wings.

Owls call in the sleep of trees.
Huddled together after a night of sex,
their wings ripple patterns in sand.

Larks rise earlier than usual,
throw themselves against weathered wood.
The old man walking out in the blue morning
finds a hundred still birds, a trail
of blood outside windows and doors.

He gives thanks for the ease of his prophecy.
The old man settles to pluck at faith—
to tell his son of their good fortune.

In days, fields are no longer
littered with bodies. The air ripples
with a silence like bird song.

Sappho receives a note from the lover
of Icarus warning her against flights
off cliffs. The envelope is sealed with wax
hardened by cold tears. She offers a feather
crusty from sea spray and blood.

Icarus's Sister

I've acquired the art to transport myself
into things. Since I first became famous for this,
I became a bulb and the earth grew over me,

the cool arms of mother swaddled me inside
my own dust. I revolved and spread before
the sun, I shot myself green, felt the heat on

my body. My brother will be the important one.
Our father has big plans for him. They coax
nuthatches and buntings into their palms to feed.

I have been pecked at while inside his hands.
His deft fingers have stroked my belly. I want
to be his twin. Before the nights shorten, Icarus

will be a sunburst. I will disappear into the eye
of one of his starlings. I want to die for him, pressed
as close as the feathers on one of his birds of prey.

CLEOPATRA'S SONG

I creep down to the Riverbanks, a long rustle
of waving stalks, ploughed and cropped under
an Archer. I lay sucking the icy tendrils of stars,
through the blackest hair of angels, knowing

I am utterly defeated, that the false housewife
Fortune has broken her wheel, that my thoughts
are prisons and these stones and funeral shells
can only witness my sharp fate, that the cinders

of my spirit will fan into a topaz evening.
I have consumed a fiery jewel more beautiful
than I. I am stricken by the sharp fangs of a clever

Master, left by this wild world with a name buried
inside my ribs. Throw my heart against flint.
I shall burst him into flame, *oh Antony, Antony*.

Katharine Hamlet of Avon Sings Herself to Sleep

She has no ambition to be their God.
They are imprinted with her kind
and this passes down through decades of nudge

and nibble. She lies in the river, vague
to any lingering passion. Flecks of silver
adorn an algae-green garland and it wraps

around her body like a visiting reveler.
Her grey eyes leak and float in the chipped
bowl of river. They lose their grip on the tender

eye sockets with their dark closets of skin. This frothy
place is haunted and despite their belief in a predictable
life, they sometimes think it's fey. A turtle grazes

her cheek, enchanted with its porcelain shimmy.
He is a practical creature and thought she was a statue,
not quite human. So many years they wanted

her to bathe among them. Breath denied them
the holiness of death. For luck, she kept a snail shell
in her pocket. She liked to stroke its mysterious entrance

and exit. A new moon will lift her body
into its silver slipper after fish gorge on her. In time,
after they shed their scales, she will be covered in stars.

Dreams of the Evil Step-Mother

I

We fought a war in the pots and pans—all the bone China plates
locked up in a graveyard of clutter, a pantry hiding bits of fur

and claw. One day, praying she'd stop tormenting my father,
I sent her away to buy sugar and bread. She stood in the doorway,

ash tumbling like snow, one red eye glowing like a demon.
She grew pale like milk, hissed like a sauce that burned a pan black.

She escaped through my teeth, swinging from my ribs. She used
my heart as a cushion for her feet. She came back though, late,

more shifty than ever. My fear lured her through the woods
back to us. My tears hit the ground and turned into pebbles

to remind her the way back like a spiteful Gretel. She stuck
diaper pins into the rag dolls I had hanging on the line.

II

She ransacked my father's chifforobe sniffing out a betrayal,
smelling footsteps in hospital corridors, a cobble-stone street

in Prague. She didn't know the truth of us, to save him I had
exchanged all the rolled up sock-fists in the house. I was desperate

to unchant her, to break her power and lull her into forgetfulness.
Why didn't I uncrown her, slip something into her lavender

brewed tea to make her leave? I'm not sure. She got older, I got older.
The Green Men in the wild woods had disappeared as my father

promised. I had nothing to play with, no real mother to confide in.

Her nails became yellow curls like wildflowers, her teeth became
dull pearls I could string and wear like a rope of garland. She
was all I had left to wound me. In the end, I silenced her perfumed

memory on the shelves along with other sordid discards.
A jar of petroleum jelly, label peeling off, some tangled dental
floss. She was like a lipstick whose color I had outgrown.

I sip her from a mason jar, secretly like broth, terrified
that in the end she's all I have left, the last trace of my father.
In the end I know she'll evaporate and drip down

the shower curtain like a witch I have willed to reign.
Through the gauzy light can you see the naked woman washing
the pink scars and seams of her body? Is that she then?

THE BEST SISTER OF WYRD

I am Darkness, beneath this burnt-out moon.
My blouse and hose fall away to the unforgiving
floor. When did we three last meet? I embrace

my other two selves. Call them Chaos and Conflict.
Make the gruel thick and slab. I never wanted
to be bad. Alas, they are stronger, they shout me down.

When I met him on his destiny horse, ready to hold
court, what chance did I have? Did I tell you, I never
intended to be bad? I shudder for the green air,

the cathedral of trees where I first became his sentinel,
perched on a ditch of rain where mosquitoes raise
their kin. I am his perfect otherwild—he doesn't know me

for a hag. We can pit our wills, skin on skin, fire burn
and rag. All those years of wearing his silk, shrugging off
her guilt when she had no will for it. Bile in her throat,

she wore his ambition like a fur coat. Call me Weyward,
but beneath it all, I am a warty girl with the want of
magic. A sylph has the benefit of smoke and ermine

while I was chosen to buzz among the roses. My Master
sees me as uncommon. Them? Those weird sluts. Whose
forbidden is this, to pounce the dark together and call it love?

Soldiers

Chile, October 1973
With a line from Pablo Neruda

As my husband lay dying, his body gathered rain.
He would have called these drops of love, squeezed
from the eyes of angels. He would have made

a romantic twist and say that sea spray is salty,
the rocks would become a mermaid's womb.
It was his habit to walk, to think, to write his madness,

his swords of love. Soldiers appeared like too-late
fireflies, carrying their torches to illuminate each pebble,
all the creeping things. I hope they shined their

faces bright, their decaying mouths, each pimple off
a cliff or tree. *Es el colmo.* My husband was dying.
When the Comandante stormed our home, demanding

my husband relieve himself of weapons, the poet calmly
announced: *look around, there is only one thing of danger
for you here, poetry.* Each day he'd walk, he'd touch each

tree, each leaf, he'd scale waterfalls and cities
until he went into heaven's exile. He returns
to the earth as rain, he would say something more beautiful.

Rain nurtures the trees of the earth, he communes
with roots and worms. This dangerous man
lies in the earth, rubbing together his sticks of love.

SHAPE-SHIFTING
(FOR FRIDA KAHLO)

Porque estoy muy sola

I

I crawl on my stomach,
crossing the sea of chipped linoleum—
scales flaking off my back.

Not the scales of truth or justice:
serpent's scales, the scales of a fish
that tempt sailors.

Snake child they call me.
I wag my ass at them—
the sky, the color of paint
under my nails.

I wag my ass at the moon
grab my cheeks
invite them in.

They will say I curse spit,
talk like a gypsy, fuck like a sailor:
the honey of my ass
a calla lily for their pleasure.

They will say I honk and bray like
a goose, my donkey buttocks
under them while we ride the moon.

II

I was fucked by a steel shaft, my first lover,
a may-pole that shattered my pelvis, spilled
my eggs, and left me broken on the curb.

They didn't shoot me like the dog which
became my destiny, didn't kill me before
I became rabid, before I frothed and barked.

I learned to crawl, learned to break eggs on my
breasts to feel the coolness of the unborn, smeared
yolks on my nipples to comfort my empty shell.

The sailors are kind to me though,
kinder than Him.

Sometimes I paint ivy, I paint brambles and roses
on my skin, and he tells me: *It is the Demerol—
Addict* — he calls me crazy.

Those lovely, lonely men who use my ass
but are kind—say I have been *away*,
have had a sea change.

III

I paint a flower around my navel,
imagine myself a woman

without scars,
without this name *Pierre*.
One sailor, a boy really, who I tell
about my babies, my unborn, never-to-be
daughters, lets me cry sometimes.

He puts his tongue in my belly and tells me
how sweet my daughters will taste, how my
belly will swell with them, how the flower
I have painted around my navel will grow.

Imagine me able to run, and I can!
I run through the woods, haunted with dead,
leering faces watch me through branches,

skulls follow me. I am beautiful in fact,
a deer, the swiftest and the fairest.
Arrows have captured me though, all those
thrusting arrows, the poisoned barbed tongues.

And the moon
wags back down at me, shows me His
ass, his spread cheeks
while I spit up at Him.

He is my large crude
canvas, created by me out of my morphine,
my crawling paintbrush.

He may teach me how to bark, to bray, to spit.

But as He is my invention,
I am his.

Christmas Tree

"Like a bird that flew, tangled up in blue." – Bob Dylan

A garland of poppies grow there —
The angry dead walk on the air.
I fear for my chest, my wizened left breast,
among them, unclothed will they care?

1.

Start with her hair. No longer platinum, she is grey
as a soldier's eyes. She has seen so many angels,
the stones of France, poppies of the brave and not so,

a thin-red line where her breast used to be. I drape
a cobweb of silver and black threads, a fierce weasel
pelt to honor all her battles. Her breasts hadn't been

ornaments or an affectation, they were snarling
forest-myths that kept her safe those years, kept her
alive and angry until now. I am carefully choosing

her Christmas tree clothes. She will join the rest of them,
she lived with spirits her entire life, kept quiet through all
their battles and now wrapped in her garland

of felt poppies, I lift her arms. Are her hands clenched
into fists or is it the dead who breathes her stiff? I decorate
her like an India purse, wild mirrors, calming blue stars,

seeded beads: she was important to the trees
in the forest, a gatherer of silver-capped acorns, golden
windfall apples. This strange death, I want to change

it. She is the apple I nibble and sniff, lonely for decay.
She ignores my wishes like she has done her whole life.
She is the hoofed forest that walks away.

2.

Angels don't smile we've been told, except the smiling
angels of France. Maybe the croissants and hot chocolate, maybe

the bombs that didn't wipe away their faces. If they flew,
they flew to forest trees that sway under

the weight of titmice. Our front porch tree is thick
with pine siskins; they take shelter in the silver needles.

I met a woman who covered her gra-mere's feet with robins,
one for each fugitive angel. They sang her to sleep

as she nodded by the fire. They sang her to sleep
and they coaxed worms to her; they planted her feet

in deep moss. There in green my love goes riding, slippered
sleep was never softer, into a silver dawn.

3. The Rabbit Mother

I am shocked to have to claim my mother's body
as if being handed a poppy by a stranger who has asked
me for a dance. I am avoiding the building
my mother rests in, the long gash of wounded red

bricks, her withered body, the plastic bag and tubes
that slither over her like ghostly snakes. I am avoiding
all my mistakes. She flickers from flame to an icy
rabbit's ear. After the hail storm that takes down the tops

of trees I catch a glimpse of her twice—in the snow
moths and the den of twigs. I call out to her *Run,
Mother, hide.* A winter rabbit waits for spring to warm
her kits' whiskers. I discover the rubble of a stone house

with its ruined garden in the woods. I dig poppies and bring
them home to soothe the soil. It must be done in the right
season or they never thrive. As I bend and beg them to stay
a stray petal wets my cheek, like a goodnight kiss.

MASK

For Paul Dwight Lampe, 1927-2013

His soul was like the raccoon that foraged
through the cans on our porch, came up to the door
begging, then swaggering into the house, back

into our lives. He was all around us, each walk
through the forest we saw him: wing for hair,
leaves for mouth, stream for skin. They told me,

we heard your father's voice last night singing,
the limb of that oak played its violin to heaven.
No one remembers his name but the squirrels

he used to feed: *Old Man, Wire Hands*. Meanwhile,
rain fills each empty shoe. A lost shoe on the moon fills
with stardust. Meanwhile, each courage teacher covers

her eyes with brown pebbles, removes a periwinkle shell
battered from tumble. A lawyer soothes his throat with honey
bees. Each day leads to the next. The tin can of peas

on the porch is licked empty. My father's soul dances
along the porch, puffs and settles. Nature's gentleman
pokes through last night's supper.

LoveSong

After reading Ted Hughes

The couple loved one another. In the beginning,
like a father, he dressed her like a doll, tied

up the laces of her boots, his favorite boots,
and tipped her velvet hat just so. She preferred blue,

he liked cherry-red, just like the scarf he tore
off her head when they met. She was the blood

on the birches; he worried the smooth bark
with his teeth. They loved to walk the wild forest,

sometimes littering poems, sometimes leaving a
trail of bones. He was the cold air she sucked

during their hikes into the mountains. They were
the bowl of steaming soup she placed on the wooden

table, the glorious golden potatoes grown in their own
garden. Each night they licked the bowls clean, nibbled

their bounty, delighted with each succulent morsel.
They put the leftovers on the porch for the raccoon.

Sometimes, the cocky raccoon cowered when they met
him on the porch. He loved her and she loved him.

The husband always bought her a green velvet hat, mossy-green,
or once, icy-sea blue just like she liked. One year he found

it mistakenly in a pile of discards, but he resurrected it,
and left it out to please her. She told him it was like a writhing

spirit rising off the bed. But they two loved one another, told
themselves they were lucky. Last night just after the hot tea he knew

she liked, they heard the raccoon. He dragged away the bones
from that night's supper, gnawed the fatty carcass of chicken.

The Ghost of Shura Speaks

Daddy, you emptied oxygen
into one of her honeycombs. I was perfect,
an amber bead on your tongue

when you kissed mummy, filled her
bones with bees. The dead are lonely.

I walk to the river and sing to you, move
the planchette among smooth stones and reeds.
The terrible smell of sweat and sweet gas,

her hand on my mouth. If I am a good
girl, I will get a butterscotch treat or a bright

mandarin orange until we sleep. I go
to the river to sip rainbows. I chip away
your name where mummy disappeared

into the earth. If you can have two little
girls, I can have two queens. The letters move

merrily and we will play until you are old
and I am no longer afraid. The rabbits I free
circle the wild fields and I wrestle

the weasel and the hawk. You are responsible
for all my other deaths. I carry sacks

of dirt into your lungs and throw you
like a curse into the Teign, Dart, Taw
and East Okement. We wait for the others.

A brother who melts the blackness of a crow,
a sister who baptizes our wings with rain.

Eating Crow

After Reading Ted Hughes

A Devon autumn chases ghosts down alleys, Shura
should have been our lost baby, the one flowering

from the toilet the day you crumpled your face, pasty-
white like the old hive, resurrected with blue-heart eyes.

I was Prospero. I was Caliban. I was the filthy-nailed
stand in for Daddy. Already, my tongue bled lies, my dick—

thick with honey, my vows of wild-escape. It was I who
bought you your Taroc pack. I, who taught you the plays

of Shakespeare, you only knew three before we met. That holy
number, that trinity of lost marriage—three meant

a witch has entered the sky. You invited her in, you dreamt
her real and she appeared, asleep like a princess-hag

in a pike's drunken eye. The wild earth wanted you back,
with all its cunning fox-holes, its voices lulling you to sleep

under the deep sighs of the house. A weasel-gypsy caught
you with her icicle fingers, calling you out of our sweet honey

moon sleep. She declared you dead: borrowed entirely by me,
not quite blue. Sycorax again lured you to her brothy-bridal

cauldron. Still you finished each poem, each postcard.
You filled each terracotta pot with earth and all your favorite

flowers. But it is Shura who makes her silent howl
while the moon fills, plump with its leaking mother's milk.

It is Shura who grasps her rag-button dolls, clutching
them to her chest like a crone-woman suckling a lost baby.

Devon Song

"Magical fear mother will become a child, my child: an old hag child."
– Sylvia Plath, January 1959

A piebald mouse has a map in the shape
of America stained into its fur. Mornings,

I turn back the clocks in our pillows,
contemplate cutting my hair into a Veronica
Lake bang. The children fuss and play.

When I suck my fingers, I am as fair
as the dollops of honey I scrape from the last

queen's hive. I watch you drive away to teach
slim hipped sophomores how to kiss, how
to parse a poem. I arrive here when the days

grow short. The women in the curled
wallpaper make me peel them back so we can

admire the straight beams underneath. My friends
are the traps I've sprung, knowing your need
for bait and release. There are rabbits everywhere,

going underground. This land is prolific.
Apple blossoms dream, twitch like dogs

in their sleep. You slaughtered a thousand
rodents for our country table. You grew my baby
in a pike's eye. The town mouse scurries, attends

to the shrike's dark larder. Our mothers leak
warm milk, sour poison from the paps of liberty.

Full Fathom Five

"Thy father lies." – Ariel, The Tempest

I take each whelk that I have picked
out alone and feel the rush and spray of some

nameless creature that once breathed inside
the ocean, like we breathed inside each other.

Irritating mollusks, they survived as something
altogether different, worn empty, not as they were,

but as undercurrents forced them to become.
I lay each thin piece of shell down like rapture

until it forms the sun. Then knowing your
undercurrents, place them into one perfect heart.

Love and spring still take me by surprise as do
their unforgiving lies. So when I lie awake

in the dark I wonder whether fools or ghouls
have destroyed that day's handiwork. I memorize

each tumbled shell that was removed and replace
it until I have invented you over and over. I've lost

you to those who try and pick our children's
pockets. Just now looking at the scurrying

creatures on the bright sand I feel each new
poem welling up, salty in my throat.

THE GHOST OF BRANWELL DRINKS BITTER
(BLACK BULL TAVERN, HAWORTH)

Everyone loves a good story, so here's mine.
You'll say I am barking but not so moony I don't know
what I am. Their litanies could make another poem

altogether. She repeated, more than once, I was the smartest
man she'd known, and then she turned cold. No,

not in death, she wouldn't look me in the eyes, she sent me
home. How could I face them? Charlotte haranguing me to fix
myself clean. Em, almost gone, traipsing the moors,

befriending rabbits and turnips: half-seducing ghosts.
They called me a broken fence, useless even to animals.

I thought of bulrushes snapping their swords, turtles and trees
talking back. Brambles snaked my ankles, thistle bound me to all
those what if's and what for's. If she'd only been a whore.

Was I rooted to this place a cracked jug without a cork,
no means to grow my life back, no bottle to shine

my eyes amber, to make me glow for her? After she refused
the sight of me, or any apology I could make, she cast me
back to my own kind. It was then I took to sucking her glass

lips, her cold indifferent tits. After too many days of this,
I confess I had my old legs back. And then the Reverend

appeared. See how he glowers at me, in the corner of this place?
Lip curled, he insists on my charity, my temperance
to forgive them all. I promised my sisters I would take none

of the bad, just enough to loosen the buttons of my trousers,
to take her legs around my waist, that frock spilled wild

across the chair. It is time now for me to return to my rest.
Another March will summon him to me, each to
the other. He, who shot his seed like a rifle into my cunt-mother.

Maybe, this year, tonight, he'll nod his acceptance my way.
Maybe his lips will brush warm on mine. Forgive me

Father, just this once for I have sinned. But what worth
is a man without a kind lady who cried out
I was made of the softest deerskin cape, the nights she undressed

for me? The amber moon averted its eyes, placing bread
on our willing tongues, giving us peace and its blessing, finally.

Shadows

"I sit in thy shadow but not alone." – Elizabeth Siddal

In my other life, I am the painter and not the model. I am not draped
in weeds with a crown of clover, there is no romance in frogs or fish,

no beauty in freezing on a bed of stones and snails. The men who
create know God. In my other life, I know the love of a few good women.

I chortle sonnets as easy as I guzzle porridge. No lectures of: *Eat,
you are too skinny, remember if I must I can paint your body thin.* It is

my face they wanted, they want. Sad that beauty weeps kingdoms from
my own eyes. I will admit I pinched this life from the street like Gabriel

clasped a phrase to his bosom. But you will have the truth,
my pleasure is no match for them. Night after night, my lover cloaks

me in a gauzy-grey gown of mist, am I not beautiful when you know me
like this? I grow cold and ugly in this Hamlet bath water. I am more than

the dripping paint off a stiff bristle brush. Night after night, I dream
of my other life as a mother. This child sleeps inside me and together we

float as on lilies towards the smooth stones of the river. No, I see
they are white stars peering at us through the dark eyes of God.

Rose La Touche

"You can only possess beauty through understanding it." – John Ruskin

Presently, the drawing room opened, and Rosie came in. Rosie or Rose, Lily or Fawn. She was not tall, nor short. She was perfect but alas a ten year old girl. I could smell her before I saw her, the tresses on her

neck. She was Rose and I was Ivy as I imagined us lying in a bed of petals. She was a Rose with no thorns, a star gazer lily and me, her new Master.

I owned her. She owned me. Living is short, remembering these moments is long. When she died horribly in love with Jesus and not me, madness turning her China-blue eyes into an empty glass, I became a broken winged

dove, no longer afloat in her eyes. I died with her. When my pet left, my innocent fawn, my heart failed to summon a correct beat, I was pebbles

of rain pouring over barren soil. My Rose did have a thorn after all, a brutal piercing of my heart. I was forbidden marriage, and always her teacher. Rose, Rose, her curled petals closed to me, I swear we never touched.

The Year Without a Summer: For Fanny Godwin

"Misery—O Misery,
This world is all too wide for thee."
– Percy Bysshe Shelley

1. The Barrier Child

It was Paris, it was August.
It would not have been raining
as they devoured one another alive
on the unbrushed tollbooth boards.

Desire and love alone stand
in need of no vindication. Some things
are our birth rights, but not death.
In the year without a summer her sister

lay with him in Switzerland, dreaming
of the way we might make monsters
of humanity. She stepped into life.

She likes to think it was raining.
It rained all night when Mary came.
It's raining tonight in Swansea.

2. Laudanum

Of course I was there to talk her through,
I loved her and she loved me.

We were scattered all over the field behind
her room, madly in bloom, bursting
up half-concealed in faith, self-made—

she'd rush at me after work, released after long hours
where I grew stronger seeking the light, all renewal,

broken up until she found me. Scattered, she joins me
to her sewing needle—my withered head,
just an achy-sweet tempered beast—

to her needle, pierced through as she sings lullabies
to cherubim and I become her, soon, a small-glazed

crock, she sorts me out. I sweat, the droplets join
the bottle head, the sugar spins me soft to rest
on her tongue. I am more than a brown field barren

through the glass, emptied of flowers. My smooth neck,
all those withered moments, I cover her slick tongue

seep through to the outside, lie down on her silky skin
in cool dirt, in blood-red slippery blossoms.

3. The Monster

"Did I solicit thee from darkness to promote me?" – Milton, Paradise Lost

It's like an old story. I am already gone. I tunnel
through the dark while our father conjures
filth around me. Mary huddles before their bonfire,
dreaming of her freak. And every day they go

sailing on wine-dark waters. In gibberish I plead,
release me, like a fish into those seas you cannot fathom.
She pieces together skin and sparks that crackle lightning,
that split the forests of Darwin. Impenetrable to love

I slip through the slender ribs of the world. I sew
a black scrap of nightmare, paste sloppy edges
to my sister's stars. I have already crossed over.
She stitches her baby from black-forest skin.

The wolves of summer scatter deep into the forest.
I spin light through glass, messages through their planchette.
A promise of oppressive love may soak through
their sticks: I announce myself to him. My lover

is a poppy; her lover is a lightning storm. As my sister
carries angels, I force words through their crystal glass.
My baby's cry wakes me in the night. I suckle
failure. I knit him from shredded petals.

Sarah Bernhardt's Missing Leg

She is wheeled in surgery humming the bars to La Marseillaise:

Marchons! Marchons!

Qu'un sang impur
Abreuve nos sillons!

Twilight sleep
    purple Iris swallowing her whole
    right leg above the knee 1915

Pain falling through a hole in the clouds, soft soft bouncing off wings of angels

light is body, light is tunnel to crawl though, light is Alice through a crooked house

where has her leg gone? Imagine the performance among cemetery soldiers, one leg able
    to dance.

  Dearest Doctor Dieu,

Beloved friend, I have only a decade left to live, I beg you, remove this pain
  let me suffer no more, I can perform with a wooden leg.

    Franco-Prussian War establishes hospital at the Odéon
performed for troops in barns and ruined villages

    ruined, I am not ruined, I am not my leg,
I am magic

1325-75; (noun) Middle English *ruine* < Middle French < Latin *ruīna* headlong rush, fall, collapse, equivalent to *ru(ere)* to fall + *-īna* -ine2; (v.)(< Middle French *ruiner*) < Medieval Latin *ruīnāre*, derivative of Latin *ruīna*

It would take some ingenuity to give an idea of the intensity, the ecstasy, the insanity as some people would say, of (the) curiosity and enthusiasm provoked by Mlle. Bernhardt.
Henry James

    I fell.

I fell from the sky like Icarus. I would never have not gone up even if it means one must come down. As for my leg, one relishes the pain.

                      Who has fallen, hell hell
              fallen from the sky, not I not I.

For Angel Claire

Oh, very well. I shall write you one last time,
as you could never read my thoughts.
While I wait for him to encircle my neck
with hands, to sharpen his blade, his lover's scythe,
I shall tell you my conscience, Angel Claire.
I shall be a truth teller, finally.

Sleeping under the trees has made me wise of you.
I asked, *Shall we meet after death?*
Yet, you remained mute. For I know now,
in the slices of darkness between waking
and dreaming, when I was free of all practical
thought, that I have wronged you by declarations,
when in fact, I have done everything with willful
consequence. I have decided, in the end,
that your presence whether in absence or in flesh
was a hollow fire, all smoke and autumn cinders
easily extinguished with snow.

And it has been snowing throughout this,
my last night on earth and I have watched
each flower blossom and fall.
I dress with care, as if my wedding day,
when I shall meet my final husband.

Oh,
what bliss to be free of you.
The ground bloody with us.

Laurie Byro

He will release me.
Release me as you were unable.
Release me to my bed of dirt and grass,
with snow a blanket covering
that rids me of this cold consuming flame
from my tedious misfortune
for having loved you.

An Ocean as a Deity

"Fear not for the future, weep not for the past." – Percy Bysshe Shelley

At night, the white caps I feared are pillows
to rest my head upon. I am content
to talk with souls who spent nine months floating
in the dark sea of Mary. *Don Juan*
is no ladies' ship splintered by romance.
These years have made me fitful with visions.
A child claps like a naked deity while friends
bloody and mangled, arrive to report my house
is falling down. This womb is crowded with weeds.
Mary will laugh to learn how I stayed alive lecturing
god about my unborn children. A fishnet will drag
me to the sands of Lerici where my heart will beat
until she finds me. It drums as steady in a gull's mouth
as in my wife's hands, when she returns it to me.

Day of the Dead

"Don't let it end like this. Tell them I have said something." – Pancho Villa

To honor him, to honor my general,
I draw a skull and crossbones
on each knee, wear my ribboned dress,
turquoise like my eyes, to the parade.

My name is Luz Corral de Villa.
My husband has been dead a long time.
He came into my mother's store
when I was sixteen and a beauty.
He demanded blankets, bags of flour.
He told my mother he would have me too,
when his revolution was over.

He kept his promise and returned,
eyes flashing fire, pockets bulging silver.
He was shy when he took down my hair,
less so when he broke me like a bottle
of his clearest tequila.
How love stings.

You will think me a romantic.
There was no time for that. I cooked
for him, I fought those who called him
bandito.

Once, a bastard patriot tried
to slit my husband's throat. It was after
a night of wild stars, too much drink.
The assassin held the same knife

held under my breast during love-play.
I took the closest pistol I could find
and shot off his left ear, half his cheek,
splattering bits of teeth.

He howled under a coyote-moon, rode
his horse clear to Texas, died (I prayed)
along the way. What good is a man
with half a face?

Children rush at me as I walk the parade,
pick at my ribbons with their grubby fingers.
They shake gourds painted with red devils,
black cats to scare away evil.

They should not fear me,
an old woman, a heroine—
married to a hero. I am
Luz Corral de Villa.

I may no longer
smell like daffodils or wet earth.
But with my general walking beside me,
I am not quite living, not quite among
the shadows.

He lives inside me and soon when
I am no longer waking, I will join him—
to sleep inside a mercenary's mansion.

Horse Thunder

For Gordon Flowerdew and all the horses

Because he shined above me like a waterfall,
giving away my last gulp of diamonds, my last
swift scepter of chance, quenching me,
I was able to leave my broken soldier in his patriot's

pants. Am I still here or was that thunder?
I have grown to believe in One greater than man,
who rolls mountain laurels back, fog and crows,
rusted machinery, heaven— not circumstance.

He who parts green mosses with his frothy arm.
Angel or Pegasus, whatever form he has driven
from the sky. I am a charred bone of remorse, gambled
by a calloused hand. We fled Moreuil to plant a forest

filled with flowers from the dew of our fallen
legs. The horse he rode flew off the bridge,
one arm stayed a swan's wing. Which God has rescued
him for this, has changed him into a silvery fish?

We have rolled the stone back from the cave. Lightning
summons red, we are a flash of speed each burying
our thin bones of dislike. Our hooves make thunder. We lament
a life that once flushed foxes, ferried revelers, all kinds.

The Girl from the North Country Speaks

After Bob Dylan

The north country woods
where I come from are gone,
a highway passes from end to end.
I am older now but I get along,
with no fires left to tend.

The storms that raged were deep and wild.
The snows made my season a memory.
Regret became a restless child
that ran in my blood and poisoned me.

I wonder if he remembers how
we prayed at night while the forest wept.
I wonder if he thinks of me now
and all his words that I have kept.

I've kept my hair both long and fine,
it misses his hands when I take it down.
For he once was a love of mine.
For he still is, though not around.

And if you see him give him this,
with a lock of my hair still soft and warm.
I think of him with every kiss.
I think of him through every storm.

George In Grackles

For George LeBlanc

"No one ever told me that grief felt so like fear." – C.S. Lewis

I am waiting for news of George's death. A dragon will get to him
eventually. As I walk in Silence, I know that all men, at some point

in their lives, are faced with unimaginable sorrow. I do believe
sorrows are winged. I do believe they are dark angels

like the black birds that descend on my path off these wintry trees.
George has lived a long time. Our trees are filled with grackles,

so many seeking to attach themselves to us.
Our trees will not shield us from these sorrows.

They are Emily Dickinson dashes -- they stubbornly dance
in the snow. They are dressed for winter, old men in sensible black

shoes. They are marching. I am frightened for George.
These feathered troubadours are writing litanies in the ice filled

forest, leaving behind their spidery farewell letters. There are too
many of them to shoo away. I leave a few behind to sip our tears.

ABOUT THE AUTHOR

Laurie Byro has been facilitating "Circle of Voices" poetry discussions in New Jersey libraries for over twenty years. Her work has been published widely in University Presses and she has been included in several anthologies. Laurie has garnered more IBPC (InterBoard Poetry Community) awards than any other poet, stopping at 55. Prior to this collection she has had several collections of poetry published: "Luna," *Aldrich Press*, "Gertrude Stein's Salon" *Blue Horse Press*, "Wonder," *Little Lantern Press*, "The Bloomsberries" *Kelsay Books*, and "La Dogaressa" *Cowboy Buddha Publishing*. Laurie has recently received two New Jersey Poet's Prizes and a *Poets & Writers* Grant. Laurie is currently Poet in Residence at the West Milford Township Library where "Circle of Voices" continues to meet. She is married to the artist Michael Byro who has graced the covers of her books and a cranky Maine Coon cat, Caliban, who is in the process of suing her for not acknowledging him in the past and the impact he has had on her world.

ABOUT THE AUTHOR PHOTOGRAPH: *Michael Byro, from a statue at Pacem in Terris, Warwick, NY by Frederick Franck*

Acknowledgments

The author would like to thank the judges and editors of venues where the following poems appeared, some in earlier forms:

"The Best Sister of Wyrd" – *Loch Raven Review*

"The Birds That Lay Down For Icarus" – "Luna," *Aldrich Press*

"The Christmas Tree" – *Journal of New Jersey Poets*

"Cleopatra's Song" – *The Peacock Journal*

"Day of the Dead" – *POETiCA REViEW*

"Deirdre Beatrice Craig" – *The Peacock Journal*

"Devon Song" – "The Bird Artists," *H & H Press*

"Eating Crow" – *InterBoard Poetry Community, Melancholy Hyperbole, Scarlet Leaf Review*

"Full Fathom Five" – *InterBoard Poetry Community, WINK: Writers In The Know*

"The Familiar" – *Peacock Journal*

"For Angel Claire" – *WINK: Writers In The Know*

"Horse Thunder" – *Peacock Journal*

"The Ghost of Branwell Drinks Bitter" – "Gertrude Stein and Other Legends," *Blue Horse Press*

"The Ghost of Shura Speaks" – *Melancholy Hyperbole*

"The Ghost Visits Gertrude Stein" – *Vincent Van Go-Gogh*

"The Girl From the North Country Speaks" – *Peacock Journal*

"Isadora at 27 Dance to Tchaikovsky" – *InterBoard Poetry Community*

"Katharine Hamlet of Avon Sings Herself to Sleep" – *Loch Raven Review*

"Lies For Icarus's Mother" – *Journal of New Jersey Poets*

"LoveSong" – *Verse Virtual*

"Mask" – *Journal of New Jersey Poets, Verse Virtual*

"Model" – "Luna," *Aldrich Press*

"An Ocean As A Deity" – "Gertrude Stein's Salon and Other Legends," *Blue Horse Press*

"A Red Scarf" – *Chronogram*

"Rose La Touche" – *POETiCA REViEW*

"Samhain Taroc" – *WINK: Writers In The Know*

"Shadows" – *POETiCA REViEW*

"Shapeshifting With Frida Kahlo" – *Unlikely Stories*

"Soldiers" – *Panoplyzine*

"Song of Heartbreak" – *Verse Virtual*

"Staying True to Hestia" – "Dedication Page" – *Loch Raven Review*

www.ingramcontent.com/pod-product-compliance
Lightning Source LLC
LaVergne TN
LVHW021117080426
835512LV00011B/2556